D0440815

Notes on the End of the World

Notes on the End of the World

Meghan Privitello

Black
Lawrence
Press

Black
Lawrence
Press

www.blacklawrence.com

Executive Editor: Diane Goettel
Chapbook Editor: Kit Frick
Book and cover design: Amy Freels

Copyright © 2016 Meghan Privitello
ISBN: 978-1-62557-962-1

All rights reserved. Except for brief quotations in critical articles or reviews, no part of this book may be reproduced in any manner without prior written permission from the publisher: editors@blacklawrencepress.com

Published 2016 by Black Lawrence Press.
Printed in the United States.

Because of Lucio
My figghiu di puttana

Contents

estrangement
from
normally

Notes on the End of the World

Cold rainy days say *Do it, lie in bed with a stranger.*
Even if a house is on fire, and a dog is inside burning, do not leave.
I could almost believe the world planned for itself to fail.
Then a wasp burrows in a fig. Then a baby is perfect
in its inability to remember.

If you are a stranger, I am a stranger.
Things are funny that way.
Chameleons trying to blend into chameleons
until the way to go unnoticed is to disappear completely.

And when the Deep South seems empty except for dead peaches
and sallow fields, it is actually full of men and women lying in bed
asking how much closer they have to get in order to define love.
It is actually bustling with elbows and knees.

There are abandoned playthings everywhere you look.
Under the bed where you lie, a tin horse on wheels eats the carpet.
Underneath your bodies, the metallic neigh weighs on you.
You could tell the man next to you about it if you knew his name.

The hives are closing their doors.
The neighborhoods are liquidating.
The birds are going out of business.
There is an apocalypse of starlings
before they are all replaced with blips.
Binary codes cost little to maintain.
Look at the little 0010 painting
an outline of a house. It is so 1001.
The spider crawling across my head
turned out to only be a small idea.

A family has taken over my old house.

They could be wolves or Smiths or a tight swarm of bees.

The asbestos siding is a hologram in the leftover sun.

At once, it is a dollhouse made of bones.

I can see through to the basement and the walls are wet

like a toe that lost its nail.

A mute boy in the room with blood on his face is not ashamed

of being a mute boy with blood on his face.

My old bedroom has become a museum of dust.

Where I used to sleep, dead skin hovers in its own trembling universe.

The sun is covered by the shadow of another wreckage.

The clothes on the clothesline motion to run away fast or to come closer,

depending on the direction of the storm.

DAY 1

In 1913, the first highway across the country was built.
From an airplane, the country was presumptuous in its tearing apart
    of fields.

I want to be a dark road.
To say: Nest, your eggs will be crushed and cooked here.

I am no place to settle.

But then one of the pigs begins to look like a man.
When it asks to cross me I don't know whether to marry it
or cook it.

I mean, there are families to be fed.
There are wedding dresses disintegrating.
There are empty beds where children used to rest.
Now they are out trying to invent a gimmicky balloon that promises
    less walking
and constant ethereal sleep—a two for one bail out.

In 1913, there were nearly one hundred years left to live.
Every house from New York to California was a shrine
to the oven, the robe, the gold-rimmed teacup.

For the beetle's armor, can you believe in falling asleep
without the television on?

For the porcupine's knives, could you believe for a second
we used to fall in love with each other for free?

Steal what weaponry you can from the animals.

From the road, I see armies of us dressed as ghosts trying to cross.

DAY 2

All of the animals are where they don't belong.
They don't know how to get to their mothers
who will kill for them and lay their dinner at their feet
when they find their way home.

I do not have a totem animal.
I do not have a compass.

There is fire in every tall building.
Eighty boys have already gone missing.

Somewhere strangers are gathering,
which could look like the beginning
of a riot.

We don't have to do anything about it.

That means that we can be happy
with bashfulness and endlessness.

The good news is there is no reason
to make the bed. Bloodwork
is another useless poem.

Whether we wanted to know it
or not, there have always been devils
everywhere.

Birds are them.
Horses are them.
You are them.

What musculature. What flight.

We gather the lizards and snakes,
undress for kinship.

What to serve for dinner with just one
white tablecloth left, no spell
to make bread infinite.

DAY 3

A coyote returns to my yard every night,
sits under the barren olive tree
and stares.

I stare back.

We talk to each other telepathically.

I lost my hunting partner, he says.

I lost my loving partner, I say.

If I could sell my eyes to a child
obsessed with outer space
and convince him they were ancient
yellow moons, I would, he says.

I would build a fire out of the money
and burn myself in it, he says.

If I could sell my heart to a surgeon
obsessed with mourning and convince him
mine was an ancient parable of wanting,
I would, I say.

I would build a god out of money
and bury him, I say.

We are both rotten and gentle, he says.

We are both animals and children, I say.

At the same time, we imagine
a dog carcass in the yard.

He eats its organs as I curl up behind it,
my bloody fingers combing its hair.

DAY 4

I'm tired of everything
and am getting old.

I'm unexcited by stealing pets
and diagnosing strangers' loneliness
by the way they move food
around plates in low-lit cafés.

If my kindergarten teacher had told me
that coloring pictures of squirrels would be the most satisfaction
I would ever know, I would have run
the dull classroom scissor blades against my wrist
until the crayon fell out of my hand.

Look, she's bleeding!
Look, she's a rose!

I am now so conscious of time
that I have no choice but to sleep
in a bed full of clocks, trying to find a way
to love their voices enough
that together we become a chord.

I've always loved at intervals.

Passion was most fresh
when temporary.

The world, in its promise to end,
has become so bland
that when I am hungry and start to eat
the thighs of a living cow,
I could swear I was only talking.

DAY 5

Every barn has become a church
to worship storms in.

If I gathered all the unsharpened pencils
from backpacks, I would build a golden silo
that worshiped lemons or sunlight,
whichever lasts longer.

The first time a boy took off my shirt
was in a tractor for sale on the side of a road.
Inside of it, we felt so human we cried.

If I told his friends about this, he said, he would die.

He worshipped me.
Until I married, I only made love in machines.

A storm is coming.
Or my grandfather is tuning his radio
from the afterlife.

If I stayed awake for weeks, I could take down every fence
left standing and build a church so large
the living and the dead could hold hands in it
as they told each other the truth.

A storm is dividing the sky into sections like an envelope.
I want to lick it and seal it shut.

I remember, though, my mother telling me about a girl
who wrote a letter to the moon every night before bed,
the same question each time: *If you can see everything from there,
aren't you the real god?* She loved only the taste of the envelope's glue
and died of hunger.

The storm is big enough to destroy imaginary churches.

An emergency announcement was sent from my grandfather,
or another sweet dead man:

*Close your doors and pile your belongings in the center of the room.
Eat your photographs. Bury your dogs. Find one object
and memorize it. This is your angel.*

I memorized ten.

Primitive vr. institutional
cultural v. civilized

DAY 6

It is no dream to live in a house
with blown out windows and molting snakes.

Any child's drawing would tell you so:
the driveway, the garden, the smoking chimney.

I sleep with a pistol between my legs so often
that any man would be a soft nuisance.

This quiet is the quiet of watching a living thing
die, when you hit yourself for having believed the heart
could ever resemble a red bird.

I would give up all of my memories of trains
if one passed through the foothills as I watched.

All to say, there is enough emptiness to be buried
wherever the weathervane stops.
There is enough emptiness to feel holy.

At night, the wind upsets the shutters, the shingles.
And although I knew a bucket of morphine
and a glass of scotch would kill it,
I killed it.

DAY 7

Somehow, we've all been given the same fate,
which means our lives are ordinary.

I can't come to terms with the fact that the astronaut who stood on the moon
and compared the earth to his pregnant wife's stomach
will die in the same dismal flames as the man who is too large to leave his house
without removing the roof and hiring a crane.

I could have spent years in bed
listening to books on tape and masturbating
until I fractured my wrists.

I could have found the similarities
between fractures and fractals and applied the math
to the unsolvable equation of loss.

I could have let my wrists heal crooked, waited
to find a man who loved acute angles over obtuse.

He would love how slivered my world is,
explaining that some spaces are fixed,
that he loved me enough to create a symbol
to stand for me.

I have spent years trying to be more
industrious than the bees.

Queen, you have no separate savior.
Honey is no longer a reasonable bribe.

Haven't you heard?
Our god is diabetic.
Arthritic.
Hypoallergenic.

Give god a reason, he'll break out in hives.

DAY 8

If I stay in one place long enough,
I will become overgrown with moss.

This is not a curse.

I will establish an address
that defines my body in terms
of coordinates on a map.

I can finally give up
figuring out who I am.

When the moss is gone
and my body longs for the same
green comfort, it will expel enough
negative desire to create a drought.

The hard wind comes
in the cracks of the windows
like Tom Waits singing gospel songs.

You pour the last of your milk
over the sill.

Each small sacrifice is rewarded
with backstage passes to heaven.

The moss is gone and a strict limitation
has been put on water usage in the home.

This is how it goes: every loss
becomes a need.

No problem.

I have enough pictures of pistols in the mouth
to make my children cry me green.

DAY 9

When I come home, my husband says
I think I married a witch.

He's watching old movies on the old movie channel,
and I can't blame him for trying to shove his life
into a simple story that dogs, in their colorblindness,
can understand.

When the world ends, I will assume what he said is true.
That my skin is made of magic, that I can turn any tragedy
into a swan.

This means that when the sky is a black tumor
hungry for more than a solitary breast,
I will turn it into licorice.

Old men and women will eat through it and say
Dear childhood, you are loyal, you have never left us.

This means when the earth cracks open and tries
to swallow us like pills, I will hypnotize it into thinking
people are made of arsenic and bleach until it stops.

My husband tells me I am a combination
of Veronica Lake and Clara Bow, which means
I am in love with whiskey and faulty hearts,
that I do not fear death any more than I fear
rocking horses and ringlets.

When the world ends, I will be trying to turn
light bulbs into hollow stars.

When the world ends, I will be curling my hair
with my husband's burning hands.

I will be on the back of a horse as if I am riding
toward some sort of ending.

DAY 10

We've been invited to a party in 1945.

Apparently, this is what happens when time announces its ending:
its labyrinthine walls crumble.
It becomes limitless, navigable space.

We can walk backward to the days we were born.
With a seismograph, we can see how little the world moved.

We can stand next to last year as if we were all people
in line waiting to send care packages to strangers.

As for the party,
we need something to wear.

We need to look real.

I must cinch my waist enough
that you can wrap your thumb and forefinger around it.

You need a single-breasted coat and a red-breasted robin
to teach you how to be the last man singing
"It's Been a Long, Long Time".

We will be so precious that we will spend the evening
touching each other's faces and drawing up plans
to build a home in the suburbs out of white picket
synonyms for affection.

In 1945, the women will be drunk in soft light.
The men will unzip their wives' dresses
as if they are dismantling a bomb,
touch their pale backs as if they are full of land
mines.

We will be the only ones not dancing
when they announce the war is over.

When they ask us how we could cry and shatter
our plates after hearing such news, we tell them
We love war, we love lipstick, we love pocket squares
and suffering. We would do anything for more
missiles, more measles, more mourning.
Sweetheart, when it's over, it's over.

DAY 11

When the world ends, I want to be sailing on a ship
that, from a distance, looks like a folk painting.

Its misshapen sails will hold my hands
and tell me *we are helpless*
against the wind. I will touch them
as if they are small bruised faces.

From the distance of floating out to sea,
I will look through my telescope to find you
and hemorrhage when I realize
I packed a kaleidoscope instead.

Figuratively, you are the stationary
blue speck in its spectral center.

Literally, you are an almost invisible
wind-burnt man standing in a ditch.

Don't blame my eyes for being distracted
by flashy patterns. They swallow
your dim blue light and spin themselves
into maps of incurable diseases.

Chances are I will never find you.

Unless I have chosen to pack my cello,
in which case I will strum one string
until it becomes drowsy whale music
and hope that you have crawled inside the body
of Moby Dick which would be the only way
you could translate my voice saying:

I am on a ship.
I am sailing toward the horizon.
I am dressed like a star—angry
and unafraid to die.
The world has been flat all along.
By the time you hear me say this
I will already have fallen over the edge
and forgotten your name.

DAY 12

Any cup of water
can become an ocean.

The ocean can be filled with girls
in white dresses
paid to act as clouds or ghosts,
whichever you find most arousing.

If you have never believed in ghosts,
start now. They are the best
at braiding wet hair and showing you
that lopsided breasts are normal.

We are so lonely that we bite
at our elbows hoping a tear in the body
will become a door to a room
filled with everyone we've loved.

We think the room will smell
like butter and wool, but it will smell
like spit and blood. It will be full
of boarded up windows,
amnesia, infection.

It is summer, but cold.
I confuse my blue lips
with death.

When the teapot on the stove starts to whistle
like a siren, I think *This is it.*

I imagine my body being taken away
by a violent rising ocean and wish
I had found a man who would have strangled me
with the ocean's same wet hands.

With minutes until disaster,
what do you gather? How quickly
can you navigate your own useless fear?

I remember what I learned
as a Girl Scout, how to survive
in the dark world alone:
pour water out of a pot,
create a current
with your nervous seizure,
do the dead man float
to make sure you are spared.

DAY 13

At night, I dream of people I have never seen.
They have ordinary names like Adam and Claire.
I have invented their histories,
which is to say they are immortal.

Adam's double chin holds so much sadness
that, when I wake up, I can't believe my family
has not died.

Claire climbs inside of me and makes me move
like I've always feared: sexual, predatory, criminal.
She gets bloody noses, is followed by raccoons.
She is a saint.

If I look at anyone long enough,
I can convince myself they are whoever you say they are.

In shadows, we can be half real
and half invention.

There is so much night
that I can't find a telephone booth to call home in.
I can't tell whether I'm an outlaw or a wife.

For all I know, my family could have boarded a bus
and driven in reverse to a crumbling temple
praying that belief in anything ancient
would add years to their lives.

A man climbs in my window with a mask of my father.
He undresses me.
I say, *Dad, it's been years since we've been to the sea.*
Will you take me there?
My nose bleeds.
He steals all my things.

DAY 14

When the earthquake hit, it was a surprise
party. It opened us like gifts. Suddenly,
we knew things.

I can teach you how to stack the cups and saucers
in the cabinet so that they don't fall over,
ever.

Broken china is so convincing in its misery
that I once glued the plates to the floor
and walked around them saying:
It could be worse.

I don't ever want to be so crippled
that, when I sleep, you sit in your car
and call strangers.

Don't ever fall.

I don't want to seal envelopes
stuffed with articles about the country's
top ten disasters and wait decades for a response
in the form of a sweepstakes
that promises we will be set for life.

When the earthquake hit, I instantly knew
death: the chandelier and clock swaying
in slow motion, the reaching out for your lover's hand
as you say *Let's get out of here,*
before the walls crumble around us.

DAY 15

I should have known the world was ending
when the carnival never left town.

Clowns and sword swallowers lay down,
made dirt angels and hoped their magic
would sprout them wings.
What a trick hovering would be.
How much quicker you can escape what you fear
when you have no allegiance to the ground.

Rows of mason jars hold no fish.
They have been eaten by the crows.
The crows have been eaten by the clowns.

No use running away.
Our invisible hands hold on to each other.
If this were a condition, it would be called Tethering.
If there were a cure, it would require a million pairs of scissors,
an endless supply of maps.

If we were loose, we wouldn't know which way to go.
We would move around each other like carousels.
The music box songs in our chests would make time stop.

The funhouse distorts nothing.
We are that contorted.
That backward
and forward.

From the top of the roller coaster,
the carnival looks like hell.
Even the sun fears it, leaves it dark.

How many broken lights and rotting elephants it takes
to convince someone that happiness is more impossible
than tossing a ring around a bottle top.

How much we would pay to get back on the mechanical horse
knowing we had to hold on for dear life.

DAY 16

I am part mountain,
part ocean.

I am part human
when I see a burnt body
carried into a lake.

I am alive if every minor chord
makes me pen a eulogy
for someone
not yet dead.

I am half mother,
half killer,
which is to say
I am a small woman.

I am part child
if I stay awake
to calculate the number
of balloons it takes
to lift a body
out of its grave.

I am part lover
if every man I'm with
is anonymous,
if I know them
only by the size
of their waist.

I am part factory,
part sane, which is
to say I cannot stop
making mistakes,
which is to say
everything is just so.

DAY 17

nihilism

I have taken flowers for granted.
New York, I should have let you

exposure

pull my pants down outside of the bar
and give a soliloquy on pubic hair.

I should have kept every part of myself
in plastic baggies.

I have run over squirrels just to see
the color red. I have lit my neighbor's

mailbox on fire to light a cigarette
I didn't smoke. I have tried to get pregnant

in order to become a laxative junkie,
to shit my soul out in public restrooms

until I fit back into my pre-pregnancy jeans.
Soul, you are that filthy. I could smear you

on a wall and stain the white paint brown.
I have taken pills out of friends' medicine cabinets

because I was hungry and thought Lithium
would make me feel the same kind of full

as the church's thin wafers. God,
I should have saved your phone number

in my Blackberry so I could prank call you
at 2am, ask you if your faucet was running.

Tell you to go catch it. God, I have taken
you for granted. I should have let you touch

my pubic hair and kept you in a plastic bag.
God, you are red everywhere. You should quit

smoking. You won't live forever, especially not
in New York. I am carrying something

inside of me that is filthy. God, I am hungry.
I need to tell you something, but am out of minutes.   *technology*

God, if I ran toward you holding flowers
and told you to catch me, would you catch me?

DAY 18

It always starts
with a storm.

Embroidered napkins,
scrambled eggs, comforters—
things that mean safety,
that mean there is nothing
that cannot be saved.

Your deaf daughter tries to teach you
sign language for *storm*.

All you see is a seizure of hands,
a symbolic trembling.

If your red-haired wife is fire,
you will burn when you touch her.

If your deaf daughter is a vacuum,
you will disappear when you love her.

The storm is where the mind ends,
where the world ends.

Doctors ask if you come from a sick family,
try to convince you that fear is biological.

You say *Insanity is only a premonition*
of the end.

You can't stop thinking about lanterns,
cots, canned beans, locks.

You cover your face, your wife's,
your daughter's with a gas mask.
Here starts the parade of the living,
the parade of the trying-not-to-die.

In the end, your wife could be a killer
like the rest of them, a single fly
buzzing around her head.

Your daughter could be the storm.
The silent beginning.
The silent end.

Paranoia

DAY 19

Oh world, end already.

I'm tired of strange men touching my body
and me not saying anything about it.

This is a modern allegory about guilt and power,
a lesson on the seniority a bowtie has over a dress.

The neighborhood squirrels have stopped digging
to the root of my plants, to the root of things.

The neighborhood cats have stopped littering
my doorstep with beetles and mice.

At the same time, we all realized
we were unsatisfied.

Men, I understand. You are tired of lifting your family
above your head like a box full of guns, careful
not to make them go off.

You are tired, each night, of your wife's body
next to you, that burden you have sworn to God
will make you happy.

Animals, I understand. You are bored
of the earth, its unwillingness to imagine
new things for you to eat. Everything
you know is ancient, which is another word
for *tired*, for *I will sleep until I hunger*
for what is unnamed.

I am tired of not knowing how to tell anyone
about my body and what it wants.

It wants to be left alone.

It wants to be its own empty field.

My body is trying to learn how to say *Men,*
I am useless, I am poisonous, I will paralyze you
until you don't know that swallowing
is the essence of survival.

World, I am tired of being the one
still alive. In my stomach, new worlds
are growing from swallowing
your old-fashioned despair.

Oh, old world. Oh, new world.

The animals have started to eat themselves.

The men cry as they learn to touch
their own bodies in disfiguring ways.

DAY 20

As the end comes, I look for everything
I've lost: cigarette case, virginity,
the importance of purple,
family.

My blind dog, psychic in his ability to smell
cancer and the sex of unborn children,
leads me.

He sniffs the pockets of coats, the pocket
of skin between my legs and explains,
in an arrangement of food pellets
on the floor: *Beware of shallow holes,*
they are like autistic children
who put objects in their mouths,
who will kill you with your own fingernails
before they will spit
whatever it is out.

If I take the ice pick out of my ears
I can listen to his reason, understand
how careless I've been with my body
and my tools.

I can count my scars on an abacus
and play the number in roulette.
When I win, I can write a book
called *Your Magic Number* that explains
how to transform the purplest despair
into piles and piles of chips.

My dog guides me to my sister's house
where we lie naked under the pink sun,
convinced that burning is the simplest penance.

I ask her difficult questions:
How heavy was your dead daughter?
Does your husband hold you without asking?
If I built a bridge named after you, would you jump
from it and make peace on the water's dark floor?

Heavy, she says.
During storms, she says.
If you came with me, she says.

Days later, I peel the burnt skin off
her back, keep it in a pile
like old air-mail paper.

This is the closest we'll ever be, I think,
this thin giving and taking the severest
kind of knowing.

My blind dog cries.

He makes an impression on the carpet
with his paw that says
In the dead cells of her skin,
I have found your family.
There is an outline of a great tree.
They are all there—roped
around their necks, hanging.

Notes on the End of the World

On the last day of the world, it rains.
The scorpions are huddling together under an air-conditioner.
Their clicking is the last music you will hear.
Your hunger is delirious.
For dinner, you eat blue bread and your throat is too thick with it
to say how pink the sky has become.
If you had a child, you would paint her room this color.
You would name her after it, tell her to become it.
Rosy daughter, you would say. *Now you are wavelengths.*
You are safe until the sun dies.

Where there is smoke, there are circles.
Where there are circles, there are drums.
Where there are drums, there are bells.
Where there are bells, there is loss.

I've pushed a shopping cart in the dark for days.
I don't know, anymore, what a day is.
My ankles are swollen like my mother's when she ate ham.
I've asked my husband to drain the water from my body
and make a small lake in my name.
I will put my germs in it.
They will build a home there.
This is either how it begins or how it ends.
Angels, this is your last chance.
You can choose to touch us one last time
and convince us we have always been holy.

Acknowledgments

Drunk in a Midnight Choir: "DAY 6", "DAY 7", "DAY 8", "DAY 9", "DAY 10"

Jet Fuel Review: "DAY 2", "DAY 3", "DAY 5"

Meghan Privitello is the author of *A New Language for Falling Out of Love* (YesYes Books, 2015). Poems have appeared in *Gulf Coast*, *Kenyon Review Online*, *Boston Review*, *A Public Space*, *Please Excuse This Poem: 100 New Poets for the Next Generation*, and elsewhere. She is the recipient of a 2014 NJ State Council of the Arts Fellowship in Poetry.